The Complete Praise Piano Player

Paul Douglas & Dean Austin

MOORLEY'S Print & Publishing

23 Park Rd., Ilkeston, Derbys DE7 5DA

Tel/Fax: (0115) 932 0643

Where a song is used under licence the credit is shown below and any copyright enquiries should be directed to the stated Publisher.

The arrangements on pages 12 and 15 are copyright. © PAWprint Music and any application for copyright used should be to the address shown.

There are no restrictions in the use of this music in the context of worship. However we would remind you that any unauthorised copying in any form of any of this material is illegal.

Revised October 1994

Cover Design: John Moorley
Notation & Typesetting: Paul Douglas

ISBN 0 86071 388 1

WELCOME TO THE COMPLETE PRAISE PIANO PLAYER !

We hope that you will enjoy this special selection of songs and choruses which have been carefully arranged to cater for the beginner and more proficient player alike. The book falls roughly into three sections (beginner/easy/intermediate) that gradually increase in difficulty and complexity.

At the start of each song we have included a tempo direction (to enable you to brush up on your Italian !) and a metronome marking. Remember, it is always advisable to try a piece more slowly when first practising it and to use our suggested tempo as something to aim for.

Fingering has been carefully included to help you, and also various directions when there are changes of hand position, for example.

The common directions are :

"stretch" - to reach a note that is out of the 5-finger position.

"squeeze" - the opposite of stretch, where we might use, for example, finger 3, then 1 instead of 2, to arrive at a new hand position.

"cross finger over" or **"thumb under"** - to enable you to move smoothly from one hand position to another, as with scales.

"move finger/hand down/up" - usually during a rest, to start the next phrase of music in a new hand position.

"change finger" - when a note is repeated with a different finger.

You will find that for interest and practise we have included melodies to be played by the left hand from time to time, and have endeavoured to retain the character and style of each song in the arrangement; from the flowing chords of "Open our eyes, Lord", to the left hand stomp in "Hosanna"!

Most of all, we hope that this collection will make well-known Christian worship songs more accesible to you, and will inspire you to worship our living God through them.

Paul Douglas B.Mus.(Hons.)
Dean Austin B.Mus.(Hons.)

Directors, Pawprint Music April 1993

CONTENTS

Abba Father

(excerpt)

Dave Bilbrough

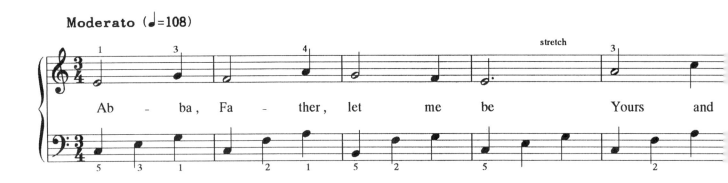

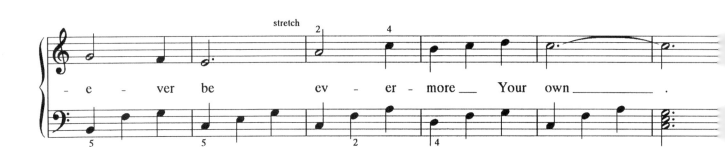

Father, we love you

Donna Adkins
Jn 12:28

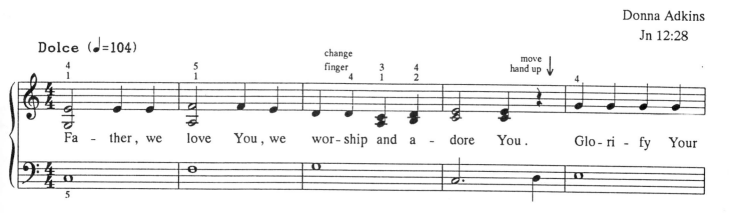

Jesus, Name above all names

Naida Hearn
Mt 1:23; Phil 2:9

Con moto (♩=138)

Je - sus _____ , Name a - bove all names _____

_____ , Beau - ti - ful Sav - iour _____ , Glo - ri - ous Lord _____

_____ ; Em - man - u - el _____ ,

God _ is with us _____ , Bless - ed Re - deem - -

change finger

- er _____ , Liv - - ing Word _____ .

Great is the Lord

Steve McEwan

Administered by Copycare Ltd. P.O. Box 77, Hailsham, BN27 3EF, UK. Used by permission.

Open our eyes, Lord

Bob Cull

Be still

Dave Evans

Largo (♩=72)

Be still, for the pre-sence of the Lord, the Ho - ly One is here.

stretch   thumb under ↑

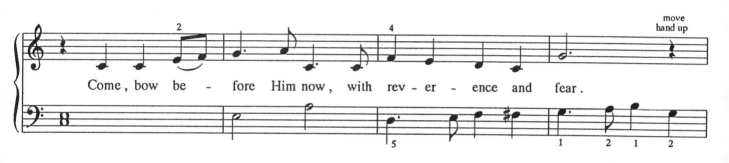

Come, bow be - fore Him now, with rev - er - ence and fear.

move hand up

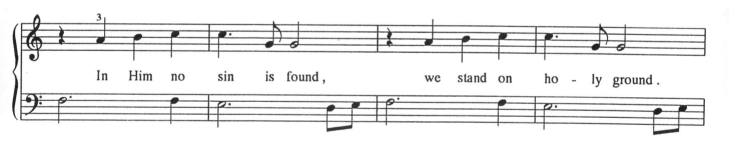

In Him no sin is found,   we stand on ho - ly ground.

move hand down

Be still, for the pre-sence of the Lord, the Ho - ly One is here.

squeeze   stretch   squeeze

O Lord, Your tenderness

Graham Kendric

James 5:11

All hail the Lamb

Dave Bilbrough

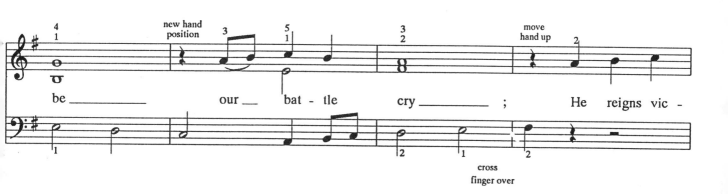

Holy, holy, holy is the Lord

Author unknown
Rev 4:8

All heaven declares

Noel & Tricia Richards

Abba Father
(complete version)

Dave Bilbrough

When the Spirit of the Lord

Author unknown
2 Sam 6:14

Con Spirito (!) e accelerando (♩=112–132)

When the Spi-rit of the Lord is with-in my heart, I will sing as Dav-id

marcato

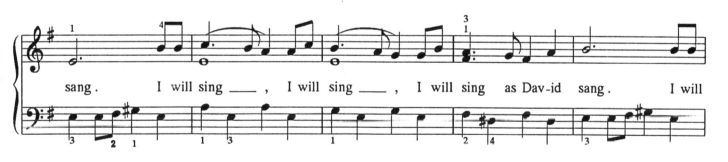

sang. When the Spi-rit of the Lord is with-in my heart, I will sing as Dav-id

squeeze

sang. I will sing ___, I will sing ___, I will sing as Dav-id sang. I will

sing ___, I will sing ___, I will sing as Dav-id sang.

God of glory

Dave Fellingham

1 Tim 1:17

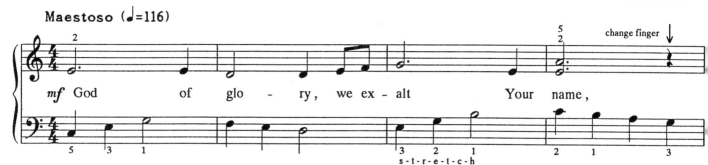

God of glory, we ex-alt Your name, Your name,

You who reign in maj-est-y _____. We

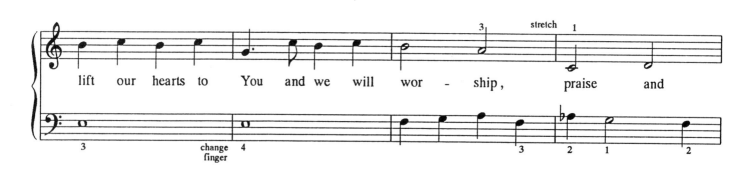

lift our hearts to You and we will wor-ship, praise and

mag-ni-fy Your ho-ly name _____. In power res-

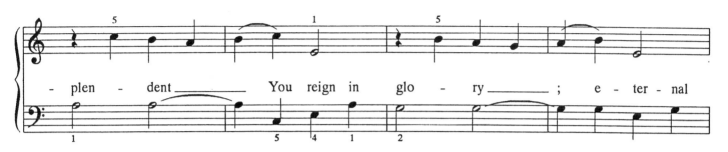

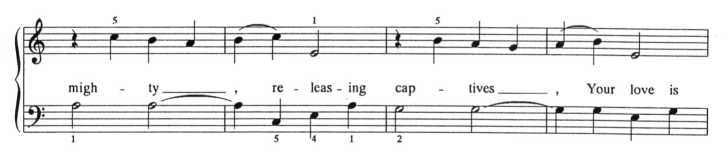

Such love

Graham Kendrick

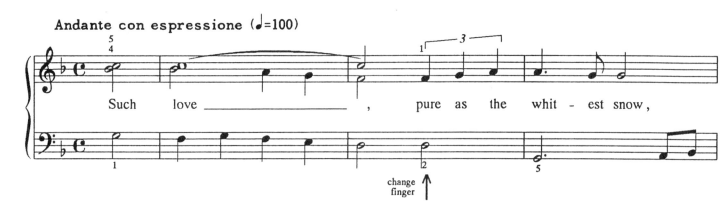

Such love _____ , pure as the whit - est snow,

such love _____ , weeps for the shame I know;

such love _____ , pay-ing the debt I owe;

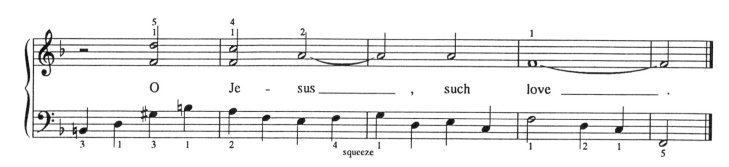

O Je - sus _____ , such love _____ .

Father God I wonder
(I will sing Your praises)

Ian Smale
Rom 8:15-16; Eph 1:5

Give thanks

Henry Smith

Give thanks with a grate-ful heart, Give thanks to the Ho-ly One, Give

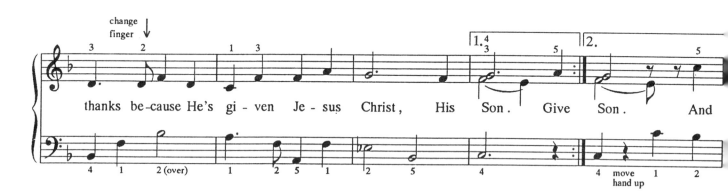

thanks be-cause He's gi-ven Je-sus Christ, His Son. Give Son. And

now ___ let the weak say "I am strong", let the poor say "I am rich", (be)-cause of

what the Lord has done ___ for us. And us. Give thanks.

The Servant King

(From heaven you came)

Graham Kendrick

Espressivo (♩=84)

From heav'n You came, helpless babe, entered our world, Your glo - ry veiled;

finger
over

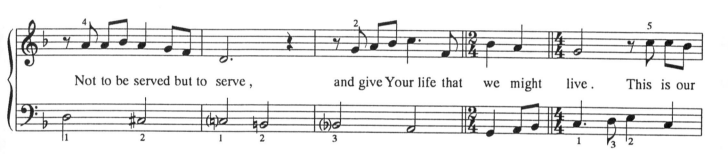

Not to be served but to serve, and give Your life that we might live. This is our

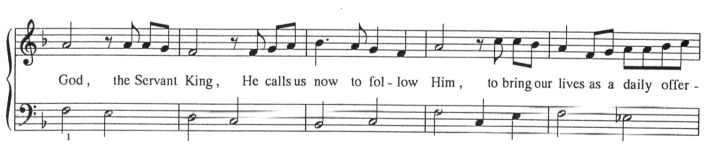

God, the Servant King, He calls us now to fol - low Him, to bring our lives as a daily offer -

move
hand up

- ing ___ of worship to ___ the Servant King. King.

stretch

Hosanna

Carl Tuttle
Mt 21:9

Allegro vivace (♩=138)

Ho - san - na, Ho - san - na, Ho - san - na in the high ___
Glo - ry, glo - ry, glo - ry to the King of

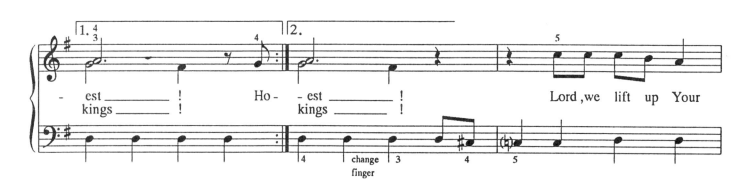

- est ___ ! Ho - est ___ ! Lord, we lift up Your
kings ___ ! kings ___ !

change finger

name ___ , with hearts full of praise ___ ; be ex - alt - ed, O

Lord, my God! Ho - san - na in the high - - est ___ !
Glo - ry to the King of kings ___ !

Seek ye first

Karen Lafferty
Matt 6:33

Con brio (♩=96)

Seek ye first the kingdom of God and His righteousness,

And all these things shall be added unto you, Hal-le - lu, Hal-le-lu-jah!

Hal - le - lu - jah! Hal - le - lu - jah!

Hal - le - lu - jah! Hal-le - lu, Hal-le-lu - jah!

My Lord, what love is this ?

(Amazing Love)

Graham Kendrick

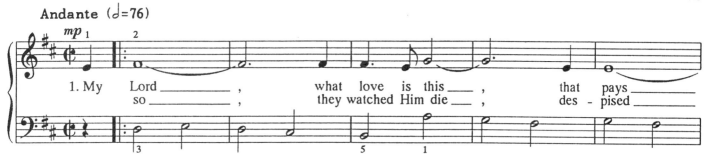

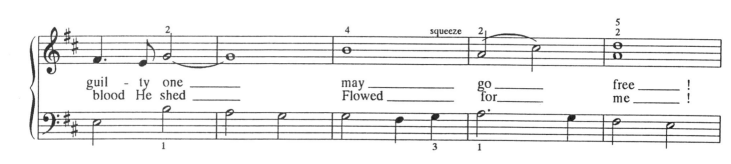

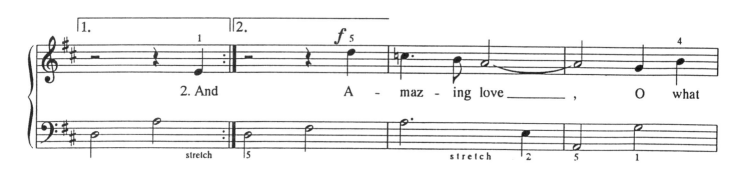

sac - ri - fice _____ , the Son of God _____ giv - en for

me _____ . My debt He pays _____ , and my

death He dies _____ , that I _____ might live _____

_____ , that I _____ might live _____ .

Jesus put this song into our hearts

Graham Kendrick
Jn 13:34-35

Je - sus put this song in - to our hearts ____ , Je - sus put this song in - to our

hearts ____ . It's a song of joy no - one can take a - way ____ ,

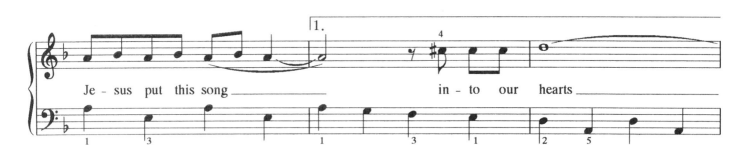

Je - sus put this song ____ in - to our hearts ____

____ . ____ in - to our hearts .

Lord, the light of Your love
(Shine, Jesus, shine)

Graham Kendrick

MOORLEY'S

are growing Publishers, adding several new titles to our list each year. We also undertake private publications and commissioned works.

Our range of publications
includes: **Books of Verse**
     Devotional Poetry
     Recitations
     Drama
     Bible Plays
     Sketches
     Nativity Plays
     Passiontide Plays
     Easter Plays
     Demonstrations
     Resource Books
     Assembly Material
     Songs & Musicals
     Children's Addresses
     Prayers & Graces
     Daily Readings
     Books for Speakers
     Activity Books
     Quizzes
     Puzzles
     Painting Books
     Daily Readings
     Church Stationery
     Notice Books
     Cradle Rolls
     Hymn Board Numbers

Please send a S.A.E. (approx 9" x 6") for the current catalogue or consult your local Christian Bookshop who should stock or be able to order our titles.